THE STENCIL COLLECTION

Traditional Borders

Maggie Philo

Oak-leaf Tile 8

Paisley Border 12

Arts and Crafts Border 16

2 Introducing stencilling

2 Basic materials

3 Getting started

4 Planning your design

6 Paint effects

7 Different surfaces

Celtic Knot Table Linen 20

Laurel and Ribbon Panel 24

Victorian Border 28

INTRODUCING STENCILLING

Once you begin stencilling you will be amazed at the wonderful results you can obtain quite easily and without spending a great deal of money. This book introduces six themed projects and provides ready-to-use stencils that can be used with numerous variations in design – just follow the step-by-step features and simple instructions. With very little paint and only a few pieces of equipment you can achieve stunning results. Have fun!

BASIC MATERIALS

Paints and Decorative Finishes
Emulsion paint
Water-based stencil paint
Oil sticks
Acrylic paints (bottles and tubes)
Specialist paints (for fabrics, ceramics, glass etc)
Spray paints
Metallic acrylic artists' colours (gold, silver etc)
Silver and gold art flow pens
Bronze powders (various metallics)
Gilt wax

Brushes and Applicators
Art brushes (variety of sizes)
Stencil brushes (small, medium and large)
Sponge applicators
Mini-roller and tray

Other Equipment
Set square
Blotting paper
Scissors or scalpel (or craft knife)
Roll of lining paper (for practising)
Eraser
Soft pencil
Fine-tip permanent pen
Chalk or Chalkline and powdered chalk
Long rigid ruler
Tape measure
Plumbline
Spirit level
Low-tack masking tape
Spray adhesive
Tracing paper
Paint dishes or palettes
Cloths
Kitchen roll
White spirit
Stencil plastic or card
Cotton buds
Methylated spirit

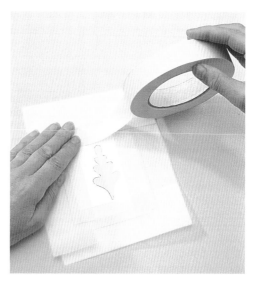

CUTTING OUT STENCILS
The stencils at the back of the book are all designed to use separately or together to create many different pattern combinations. Cut along the dotted lines of the individual stencils and make sure you transfer the reference code onto each one with a permanent pen. Carefully remove the cut-out pieces of the stencil. Apply 50 mm (2 in) strips of tracing paper around the edges using masking tape; this will help to prevent smudging paint onto your surface.

REPAIRING STENCILS
Stencils may become damaged and torn from mishandling or if the cut-outs have not been removed carefully, but they are easy to repair. Keeping the stencil perfectly flat, cover both sides of the tear with masking tape. Then carefully remove any excess tape with a scalpel.

GETTING STARTED

DUPLICATING STENCILS

Stencil plastic (mylar) can be used; or card wiped over with linseed oil, which left to dry will harden and make the surface waterproof. Place the cut-out stencil on top. Trace around carefully with a permanent pen inside the cut-out shapes. Cut along the lines with a scalpel and remove the pieces. You may prefer to trace on top of the design, then transfer your tracing onto card.

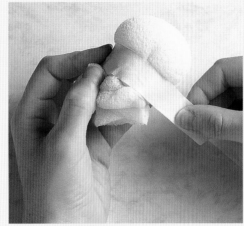

MAKING A SPONGE APPLICATOR

Sponging your stencil is one of the easiest methods, but you may prefer to use a stencil brush, especially for fine detail. Using a piece of upholstery foam or dense bath sponge, cut pieces 12–50 mm ($\frac{1}{2}$–2 in) wide and 50 mm (2 in) long. Hold the four corners together and secure with tape to form a pad. You can also round off the ends with scissors or a scalpel and trim to a smooth finish. The small-ended applicators can be used for tiny, intricate patterns.

HOW TO USE WATER-BASED PAINT

Water-based paints are easy and economical to use and have the advantage of drying quickly. For professional-looking stencils, do not load your sponge or brush too heavily or you will not achieve a soft, shaded finish. Paint that is too watery will seep under the stencil edges and smudge. If the paint is too heavy you will obtain a heavy block effect rather than the soft stippling you require.

LOOKING AFTER STENCILS

Stencils have a long life if cared for correctly. Before cleaning make sure you remove any tape or tracing paper that has been added. Remove any excess paint before it dries, and wipe the stencil with a damp cloth every time you use it. If water or acrylic paint has dried and hardened, soften it with water and ease it off gently with a scalpel. Then use a small amount of methylated spirit on a cloth to remove the rest. An oil-based paint can simply be removed by wiping over the stencil with white spirit on a cloth. Stencils should be dried thoroughly before storing flat between sheets of greaseproof paper.

HOW TO USE OIL STICKS

Oil sticks may seem expensive but in fact go a long way. They take longer to dry, allowing you to blend colours very effectively. Oil sticks are applied with a stencil brush and you need to have a different brush for each colour. Break the seal as instructed on the stick and rub a patch of the colour onto a palette, allowing space to blend colours. As the stencil sticks dry slowly, you need to lift the stencil off cleanly and replace to continue the pattern.

PRACTISING PAINTING STENCILS

Roll out some lining paper onto a table and select the stencil you wish to practise with. Using spray adhesive, lightly spray the back of your stencil and place it into position on the paper. Prepare your paint on a palette. Dab your sponge or brush into the paint and offload excess paint onto scrap paper. Apply colour over the stencil in a light coat to create an even stippled effect. You can always stencil on a little more paint if a stronger effect is needed, but if you over apply it in the first place it is very difficult to remove. Keep separate sponges for different colours.

PLANNING YOUR DESIGN

Before starting to stencil, take time to plan your design. Decide where you want to use the patterns, then work out how to position the stencils so that the design will fit around obstacles such as doorways and corners. The techniques shown here will help you to undertake the job with a systematic approach.

PUTTING PATTERN PIECES TOGETHER

1 Before you apply your design, stencil a sample onto lining paper. Mark the centre and baseline of the design on the paper and put together your pattern pieces. You can then work out the size of the design, how it will fit into the space available and the distance required between repeats.

2 You can avoid stencilling around a corner by working out the number of pattern repeats needed and allowing extra space either between repeats or within the pattern. Creating vertical lines through the pattern will allow you to stretch it evenly.

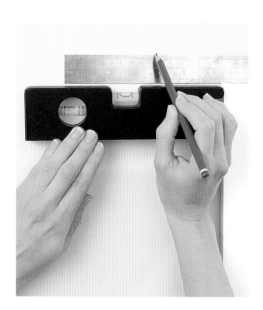 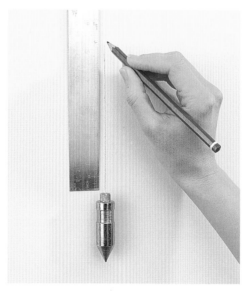 

MARKING BASELINES AND HORIZONTAL LINES

Select your stencil area and take a measure from the ceiling, doorframe, window or edging, bearing in mind the depth of your stencil. Using a spirit level, mark out a horizontal line. You can then extend this by using a chalkline or long ruler with chalk or soft pencil.

MARKING VERTICAL LINES

If you need to work out the vertical position for a stencil, hang a plumbline above the stencilling area and use a ruler to draw a vertical line with chalk or a soft pencil. You will need to use this method when creating an all-over wallpaper design.

FIXING THE STENCIL INTO PLACE

Lightly spray the back of the stencil with spray adhesive, then put it in position and smooth it down carefully. You can use low-tack masking tape if you prefer, but take care not to damage the surface to be stencilled; keep the whole stencil flat to prevent paint seeping underneath.

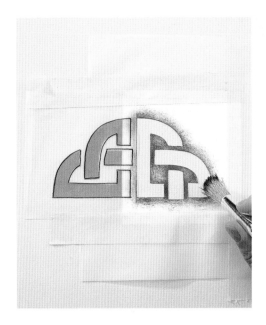

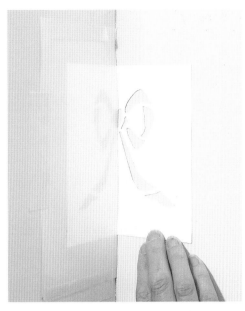

MARKING THE STENCIL FOR A PATTERN REPEAT

Attach a border of tracing paper to each edge of the stencil. Position the next pattern and overlap the tracing paper onto the previous design, tracing over the edge of it. By matching the tracing with the previous pattern as you work along you will be able to align and repeat the stencil at the same intervals.

COPING WITH CORNERS

Stencil around corners after you have finished the rest of the design, having measured the correct space to leave for the corner pattern before you do so. Then bend the stencil into the corner and mask off one side of it. Stencil the open side and allow the paint to dry, then mask off this half and stencil the other part to complete the design.

MASKING OFF PART OF A STENCIL

Use low-tack masking tape to mask out small or intricate areas of stencil. You can also use ordinary masking tape, but remove excess stickiness first by peeling it on and off your skin or a cloth once or twice. To block off inside shapes and large areas, cut out pieces of tracing paper to the appropriate size and fix them on top with spray adhesive.

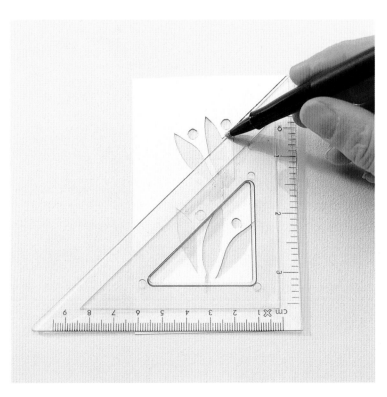

MITRING STENCIL PATTERNS

1 When you are stencilling a continuous pattern and need to make a corner, mask off the stencil by marking a 45-degree angle at both ends of the stencil with a permanent pen. Mask along this line with a piece of masking tape or tracing paper.

2 Make sure the baselines of the stencil on both sides of the corner are the same distance from the edge and that they cross at the corner. Put the diagonal end of the stencil right into the corner and apply the paint. Turn the stencil sideways to align with the other diagonal end of the stencil and turn the corner.

PAINT EFFECTS

CHOOSING COLOURS

Take care to choose appropriate colours to create the effect you want. Stencil a practice piece onto paper and try a variation of colours to ensure you are pleased with the result. Different colours can make a design look entirely different. Use spray adhesive to fix your practice paper onto the surface on which you wish to produce the design so that you can assess its effect before applying the stencil.

APPLYING WATER-BASED COLOURS

Water-based paint dries quickly, so it tends to layer rather than blend. It is best applied by using a swirling movement or gently dabbing, depending on the finished effect you wish to create. Once you have applied a light base colour, you can add a darker edge for shading. Alternatively, leave some of the stencil bare and add a different tone to that area to obtain a shaded or highlighted appearance.

BLENDING OIL-STICK COLOURS

Oil sticks mix together smoothly and are perfect for blending colours. Place the colours separately on your palette and mix them with white to obtain a variety of tones or blend them together to create new colours. You can also blend by applying one coat into another with a stippling motion while stencilling. Blending looks most effective when applying a pale base coat, then shading on top with a darker colour.

HIGHLIGHTING

A simple way to add highlighting to your design is first to paint in your stencil in a light tone of your main colour, then carefully lift the stencil and move it down a fraction. Then stencil in a darker shade; this leaves the highlighted areas around the top edges of the pattern.

GILDING

After painting your stencil, use gold to highlight the edges. Load a fine art brush with gold acrylic paint and carefully outline the top edges of the pattern. Use one quick brush stroke for each pattern repeat, keeping in the same direction. Other methods are to blow bronze powder onto the wet paint, draw around the pattern with a gold flow pen, or smudge on gilt wax cream, then buff to a high sheen.

APPLYING SPRAY PAINTS

Spray paints are ideal on glass, wood, metal, plastic and ceramic surfaces. They are quick to apply and fast drying, but cannot be blended, although you can achieve subtle shaded effects. Apply the paint in several thin coats. Mask off a large area around the design to protect it from the spray, which tends to drift. Try to use sprays out of doors or in a well-ventilated area. Some spray paints are non-toxic, making them ideal for children's furniture.

DIFFERENT SURFACES

BARE WOOD

Rub the wood surface down to a smooth finish. Then fix the stencil in place and paint with a thin base coat of white so that the stencil colours will stand out well when applied. Leave the stencil in place and allow to dry thoroughly, then apply your stencil colours in the normal way. When completely dry you can apply a coat of light wax or varnish to protect your stencil.

STAINED WOOD

If you are staining wood or medium-density fibreboard (MDF) prior to stencilling, you have a choice of many different wood shades as well as a wide range of colours. If the base coat is dark, stencil a thin coat of white paint on top. Apply your stencil and protect with a coat of clear varnish when it is completely dry.

FABRIC

Use special fabric paint for stencilling on fabric and follow the manufacturer's instructions carefully. Place card or blotting paper behind the fabric while working and keep the material taut. If you are painting a dark fabric, best results are achieved by stencilling first with white or a lighter shade. Heat seal the design following the manufacturer's instructions.

CERAMICS

Use special ceramic paints to work directly onto glazed ceramic tiles and unglazed ceramics such as terracotta. Make sure all surfaces are clean so that the stencils can be fixed easily. Apply the paint with a brush, sponge, spray or mini-roller. Ceramic paints are durable and washable, and full manufacturer's instructions are given on the container.

GLASS

Before applying the stencil, make sure the glass is clean, spray on a light coat of adhesive and place the stencil in position. Spray on water-based or ceramic paint, remove the stencil and allow to dry. If you wish to stencil drinking glasses, use special non-toxic and water-resistant glass paints. An etched-glass look with stencils on windows, doors and mirrors can be achieved with a variety of materials.

PAINTED SURFACES

Stencils can be applied to surfaces painted with matt, satin or vinyl silk emulsion, oil scumble glazes, acrylic glazes and varnishes, and to matt wallpaper. If you wish to decorate a gloss surface, stencil first with an acrylic primer, leave to dry and then stencil the colours on top. Surfaces to be stencilled need to be smooth so that the stencil can lay flat.

OAK-LEAF TILE

The design of the tiles is based on an old English pattern – acorns have been added to make the stencil more versatile. The strong colour gives a contemporary feel and would go well in a kitchen alongside traditional blue and white china. The pattern can be stencilled onto inexpensive new tiles using baked-on ceramic paint as shown here, or it can revamp existing tiles using cold-cure ceramic colour. You could also create a mock tile effect on a plain wall by painting fine pale beige lines around the design to look like grout.

PAINT COLOUR GUIDE

Ultramarine blue

STENCILLING CERAMIC TILES

1 Wash the tiles with detergent and water to make sure that they are clean and grease free, and then mark the middle of each of the tiles' side-edges with a chinagraph pencil.

2 Start with the central motif first (stencil B) and draw a vertical line down the centre and a horizontal line across the middle of the stencil card. This will enable you to line up the stencil on the tile. Next, apply the paint through this section of the stencil, then complete the corner sections (stencils A and C) and finally the curved design (stencil J).

3 When the paint has dried, bake in an oven following the manufacturers' instructions and fix tiles onto the wall.

PROJECT PATTERN

This arrangement forms the tile pattern as shown in the photograph opposite.

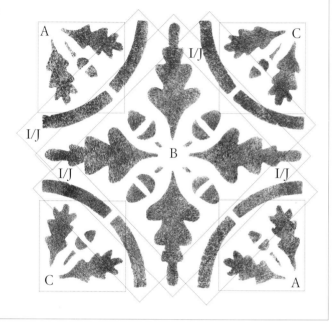

LINING UP THE STENCIL
To make it easier to line up the stencil and tile, draw a horizontal line through a vertical line on a piece of paper and place the tile over this so that the marks on the tile align with those on the paper. Then position the stencil over the tile.

EXPERIMENTING WITH THE PAINT
Ceramic paint can be fairly translucent. Try experimenting by applying paint onto a blank tile, so that you can judge the amount of paint and pressure required to achieve the effect you want.

SPONGING ON PAINT
A sponge dabber has been used to apply the paint to the tile and each area is dabbed several times to build a strong colour. You can make your own sponge applicator as shown on page 3.

OAK-LEAF TILE VARIATIONS

Oak leaves and acorns have been popular motifs over the centuries and continue to appeal today. The attractively shaped leaves lend themselves very well to creating simple traditional country designs. The rather bright oranges and pinks that have been used to create some of the variations are a twist on the russet shades seen on autumn leaves and provide a very modern and cheerful alternative to blues and whites.

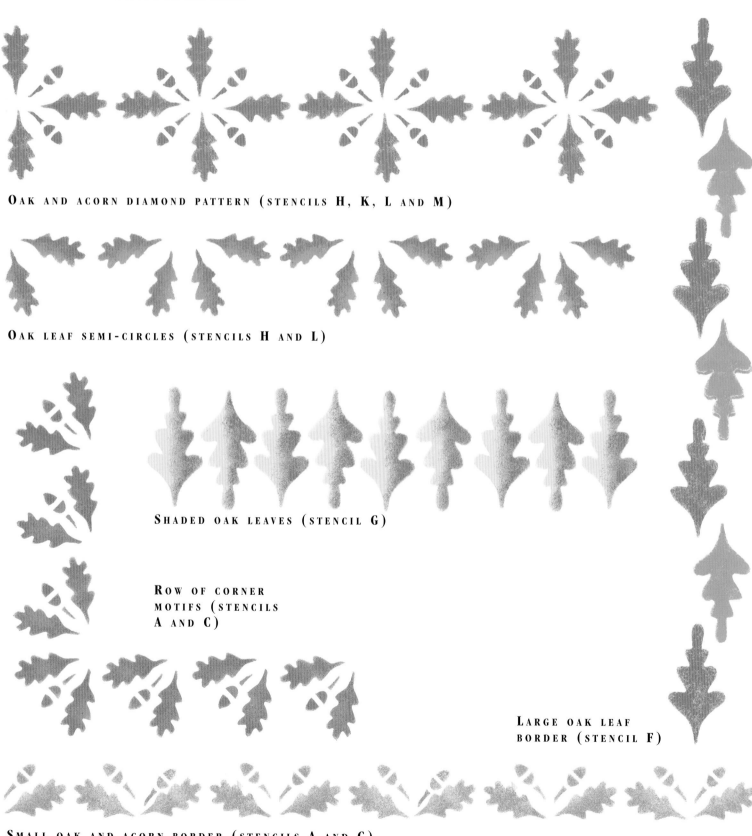

OAK AND ACORN DIAMOND PATTERN (STENCILS H, K, L AND M)

OAK LEAF SEMI-CIRCLES (STENCILS H AND L)

SHADED OAK LEAVES (STENCIL G)

ROW OF CORNER MOTIFS (STENCILS A AND C)

LARGE OAK LEAF BORDER (STENCIL F)

SMALL OAK AND ACORN BORDER (STENCILS A AND C)

OAK AND ACORN FRIEZE (STENCILS E AND F)

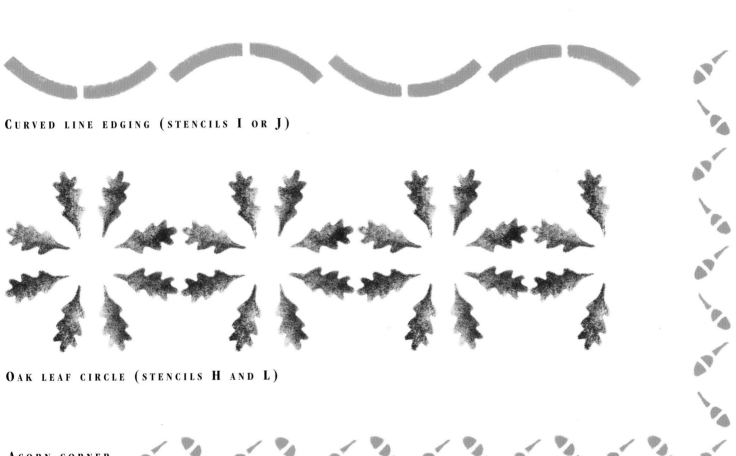

CURVED LINE EDGING (STENCILS I OR J)

OAK LEAF CIRCLE (STENCILS H AND L)

**ACORN CORNER
(STENCIL M)**

OAK AND SEMI-CIRCLE FRIEZE (STENCILS D, E, F, AND I OR J)

OAK LEAF EDGING (STENCILS F AND G)

PAISLEY BORDER

This traditional Indian motif works well with ethnic – style furnishings. The design was placed over a brightly colourwashed border – precise measurements were not used. The curtain incorporates various elements of the design, placed at random. The overall effect of both border and curtain is free and informal. When you stencil around a window, you do not need to use spirit levels and plumb lines to mark the border position – simply work at an even distance from the surround.

PAINT COLOUR GUIDE

Maroon   Ultramarine blue   Gold

PAINTING WALLS AND CURTAINS

1 Paint the wall pale pink. Mask off a border around the window measuring approximately 10 cm (4 in) wide. Mix a deep pink emulsion with acrylic glaze, following the manufacturer's instructions. Brush this within the masked area and leave to dry thoroughly.

2 Start on the outer section of the paisley design with the maroon paint (stencil B) and when you have completed all of these, place the central motif (stencil E) inside each one and stencil with the blue paint.

3 Stencil the curtain at random with gold fabric paint and iron on the back to seal.

PROJECT PATTERN

One stencil design is placed inside another to create the paisley pattern. The pattern was rotated approximately 180 degrees on alternate placements to create the border around the window in the photograph opposite.

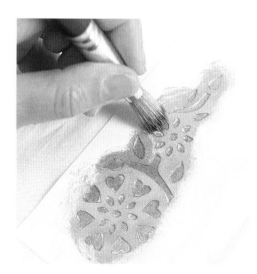

PLANNING YOUR WALL DESIGN
An easy way to plan the position of your paisley motifs is to stencil the design onto a piece of paper three or four times and then photocopy the sheet. Cut roughly around each one and use a repositional spray adhesive to attach them to the wall. Simply remove one at a time and position the stencil in place.

POSITIONING YOUR STENCIL
You can position the second stencil accurately inside the first by lining up the top and tail pieces of the design. It doesn't matter if a little of the blue paint spreads over these areas, but mask them off after positioning if you don't want this to happen.

CREATING YOUR CURTAIN DESIGN
Use a selection of the motifs from the stencil sheet to create a random effect over your curtain. You can use the photocopy technique explained in 'Planning your wall design' to plan each position.

PAISLEY BORDER VARIATIONS

Many traditional Indian designs consist of a variety of stylized flower- and leaf-shaped patterns arranged into the familiar paisley shape. The simple motifs that are contained within the design can be used in a number of different ways to create a variety of borders, all-over designs and random patterns. They can also be extremely useful for providing both formal and informal stencilled effects.

FLORAL STRIPE (STENCIL A AND CENTRE OF STENCIL A)

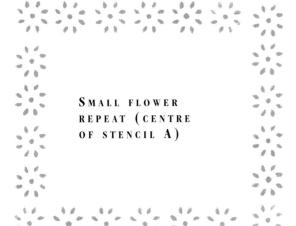

SMALL FLOWER REPEAT (CENTRE OF STENCIL A)

FLORAL PATTERN (STENCIL A)

REPEAT PATTERN (STENCILS C AND D)

BORDER WITH INVERTED MOTIFS (STENCIL F)

FLORAL CORNER (STENCIL A)

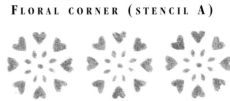

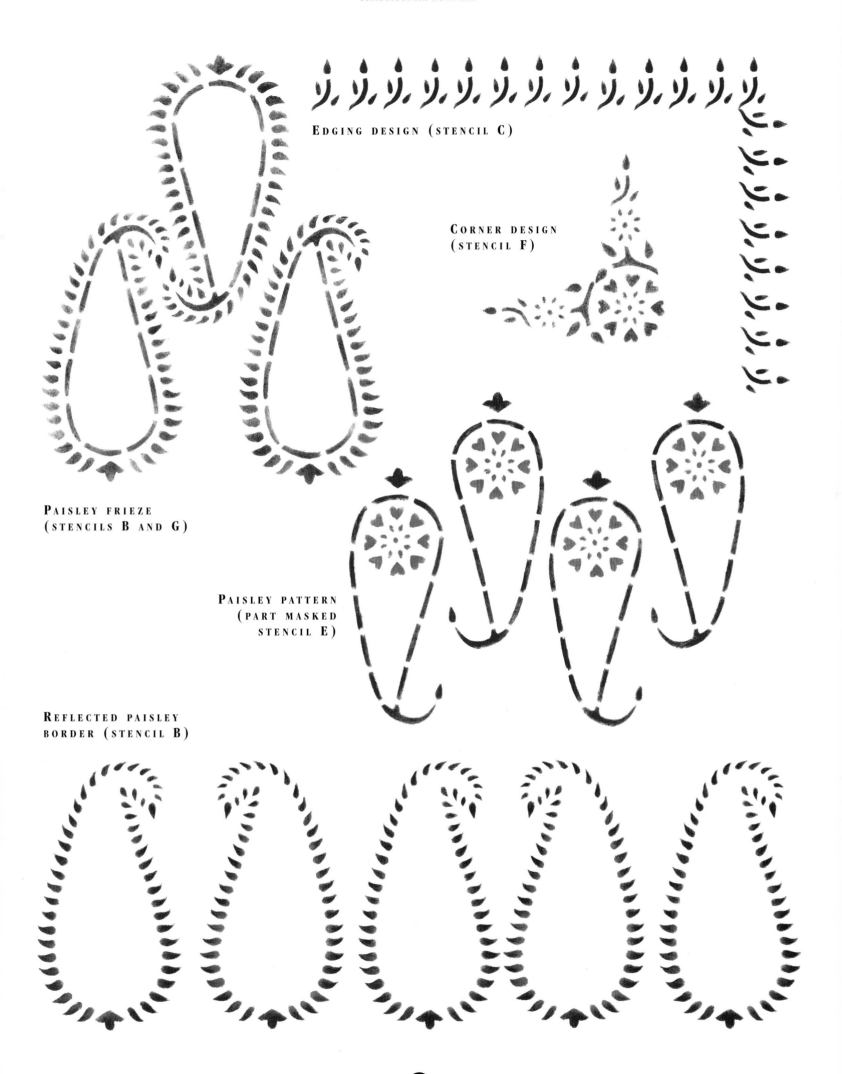

EDGING DESIGN (STENCIL C)

CORNER DESIGN (STENCIL F)

PAISLEY FRIEZE (STENCILS B AND G)

PAISLEY PATTERN (PART MASKED STENCIL E)

REFLECTED PAISLEY BORDER (STENCIL B)

ARTS AND CRAFTS BORDER

The design for this border was inspired by a turn of the century textile pattern. Although brightly coloured, it is a fairly formal design that would look particularly appropriate in an Edwardian terrace hallway. The different flowers have been placed within a trellis pattern, but you could choose to use just one of these if you were stencilling a small area. A shaded effect has been used to give additional dimension to the design – dark colours are applied on top of paler colours to create this effect.

PAINT COLOUR GUIDE

Pale lime green   Olive green   Bright red

Bright yellow   Viridian green

DECORATING THE WALLS

1 Use an off-white emulsion paint for the wall above the dado and a deep red paint on embossed wallpaper below.

2 Start by using the pale lime green to stencil the trellis design (stencils A, B and C). Use the olive green over this to give a shaded effect.

3 Stencil bright yellow paint through the flower and leaf designs (stencils D–M). Mask off flower heads (stencils D and F) in the appropriate place and stencil these with bright red paint. Use viridian green paint to colour the leaves and stems.

PROJECT PATTERN

The border in the photograph opposite is a repeat pattern of this arrangement.

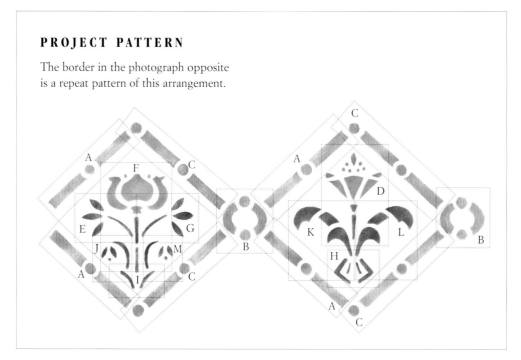

ADAPTING YOUR STENCIL
This stencil has been divided into a large number of sections to make it versatile. If you wish to simplify your design, you can make your own stencil. Use tracing paper and a pencil to trace inside each stencil.

CUTTING OUT YOUR STENCIL
Place a piece of stencil film or acetate over the tracing and use a permanent marker to trace the design in the relevant position. Cut out the completed stencil pattern.

CREATING A SHADED EFFECT
A yellow basecoat has been applied to the central design to achieve a shaded effect. This colour is particularly effective beneath flowers and foliage patterns.

ARTS AND CRAFTS BORDER VARIATIONS

This versatile stencil pattern contains lots of little designs that would be ideal for using on smaller projects throughout the home. You could try stencilling some of the flower or leaf designs onto your picture frames, lampshades, boxes, containers or stationery. The stencils below have been painted in citrus lime and orange shades to replace the yellow and more subdued greens used in the main project. They provide a bright and zingy alternative.

FLOWER DESIGN REPEAT (STENCILS D, E, G AND I)

LEAVES USED AS FLOWERS (STENCILS G AND E)

ZIG-ZAG STRIPE (STENCIL C)

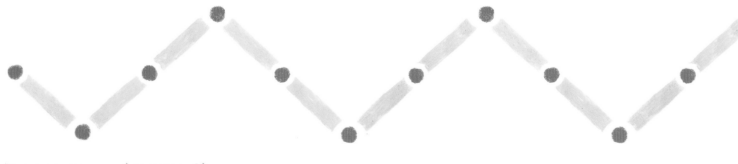

REPEAT PATTERN (STENCILS I, J AND M)

ABSTRACT BORDER (STENCIL H)

LEAF BORDER (STENCILS K AND L)

ABSRTACT STRIPE CORNER PATTERN (STENCIL B)

DIAMOND FRIEZE (STENCILS A AND C)

LEAF REPEAT (STENCIL G)

DECORATIVE BORDER (STENCILS A, C, PART OF STENCIL D, J, K AND L)

CELTIC KNOT TABLE LINEN

Both the border design and central motifs on the table linen are adapted from Celtic knot patterns. This type of non-figurative pattern is very versatile and suits both traditional and contemporary decorating schemes. A combination of charcoal grey and silver paint were used to create a pewter effect – spray paint made up the base colour and silver metallic powder mixed with an acrylic fabric medium formed the highlights. Spray paints can be washed in a cool wash and will fade gently fade each time to produce a lovely soft worn effect. If you want to maintain a crisp finish, use fabric paints throughout.

PAINT COLOUR GUIDE

Charcoal grey   Silver

DECORATING TABLE LINEN

1 Mark out the position of the border around the table linen, using masking tape to mark the top and bottom edges. Fold the linen in four to find the centre point of the cloth and mark with tailor's chalk.

2 Apply grey paint to both the border (stencil B or C) and central motifs (stencil I or A) and leave to dry.

3 Highlight the design by going over the grey paint with silver. Iron the reverse side of the linen to seal the paint.

PROJECT PATTERN

The pattern on the napkin and tablecloth in the photograph opposite uses different scales of the same design. The stencilling around the edges is a simple repeat of this border pattern. The central design uses a single motif rotated consecutively at 45 degrees, forming a circular pattern.

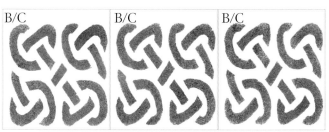

MASKING AROUND YOUR STENCIL
To protect the table linen from unwated spray paint and to prevent particles creeping under the stencil, use a repositional adhesive to fix the stencil to the fabric. Mask around the stencil, using large pieces of paper attached with masking tape.

CONTROLLING YOUR SPRAY
A sheet of paper can be held close to the stencil in order to create a barrier. This will help to contain the paint and deflect the spray onto the stencilled surface.

USING A BRUSH TO PAINT HIGHLIGHTS
Use a brush to stencil the silver highlights because this will enable you to apply the colour to the raised surface of textured fabric only, providing a subtle contrast of colours.

CELTIC KNOT TABLE LINEN VARIATIONS

As an alternative to the cool pewter shades that were stencilled onto the table linen in the main project, beautifully warm natural earth colours have been combined or used alone to create the ideas illustrated on these pages. The Celtic knot patterns are all geometric and fairly rigid and particularly suit being used as borders. You can use either the small- or large-scale designs to create all of these different variations.

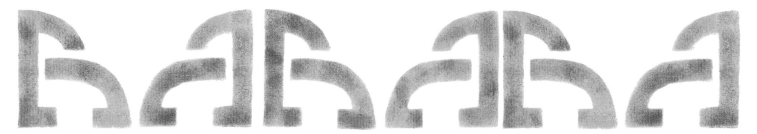

REFLECTED MOTIFS (MASKED OFF SECTION OF STENCIL A)

ABSTRACT DESIGN (MASKED OFF SECTION OF STENCIL A)

OVAL FRIEZE (MASKED OFF SECTION OF STENCIL A)

BORDER DESIGN (STENCIL D)

REFLECTED PATTERN (MASKED OFF SECTION OF STENCIL C)

ZIG-ZAG STRIPE (MASKED OFF SECTION OF STENCIL C)

**CORNER DESIGN
(STENCIL H)**

SPIRAL REPEAT (STENCIL D)

ZIG-ZAG BORDER (STENCIL E)

DIAMOND PATTERN (STENCIL E)

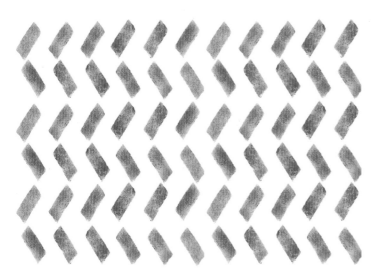

**DIAGONAL STRIPE EDGING
(STENCIL E)**

**OVAL FRIEZE (MASKED OFF SECTION OF STENCIL A
AND STENCIL E)**

**EDGING PATTERN (MASKED
OFF SECTION OF STENCIL A)**

PAINT COLOUR GUIDE

Duck-egg blue   Bronze yellow

DECORATING THE WALL

1 Paint the wall above the dado with pale blue emulsion paint and the wall below it with duck egg blue. Paint the dado rail and skirting board with a cream coloured paint, and brush an off-white woodwash colour onto the floor boards.

2 Draw a line lightly with a pencil, where the top section of the design will be placed. Draw a vertical line through the centre of this. Use a spirit level and plumb line to make sure both lines are straight.

3 Start by stencilling the bow first (stencil A), then work outwards in each direction for the required distance. Drop a plumb line to mark the position of the sides of the panel. When these are complete, mark the base of the panel and complete the design.

LAUREL AND RIBBON PANEL

The form and colouring of this laurel and ribbon panel are influenced by the Swedish neo-classical style of decoration. The border pattern can easily be extended both width and lengthways so that the panel is appropriately proportioned for the area it is to be applied to. A border of laurel leaves, without the ribbon, has been stencilled onto the woodwashed floor, giving it a simple but elegant appearance.

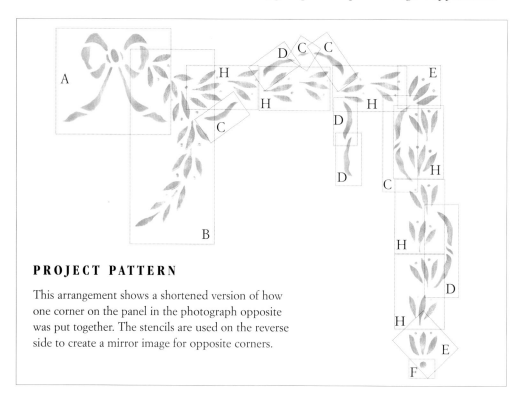

PROJECT PATTERN

This arrangement shows a shortened version of how one corner on the panel in the photograph opposite was put together. The stencils are used on the reverse side to create a mirror image for opposite corners.

POSITIONING YOUR STENCIL ACCURATELY

You will find it easier to position your stencil accurately if you draw horizontal and vertical lines through the bow and a line through the centre of the laurel leaves. You can then line these up with the lines on the wall.

STENCILLING ROUND A CORNER

Stencil the laurel border until you reach the position where you want to place the corner and drop a plumb line from this point. This is easier than working out in advance where the line should be drawn.

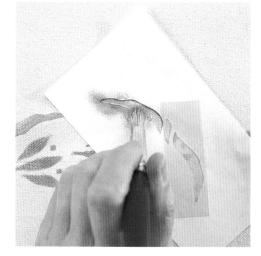

CREATING THE RIBBON EFFECT

You will need to mask off sections of the ribbon design (stencils C and D) to stencil the flowing ribbon at the top off the panel.

LAUREL AND RIBBON PANEL VARIATIONS

The traditional and subtle duck-egg blue and ochre yellow that were used in the stencils for the main project have been replaced here by an equally pretty but more contemporary yellow and turquoise colour scheme. The stylized laurel leaves can be arranged in such a way that they look like petals around a flower and the wreath can be used to create a flowing design as opposed to the static arrangement on the panel.

BOW (STENCIL A WITH END MASKED OFF)

LAUREL STRIPE (STENCILS G OR H)

LAUREL WREATH (MASKED OFF SECTION OF STENCIL B AND STENCIL F)

FLOWING BORDER (MASKED OFF SECTION OF STENCIL B)

LAUREL AND RIBBON FRIEZE (STENCILS D AND G OR H)

BOW AND RIBBON PATTERN (STENCIL A WITH THE ENDS MASKED OFF AND STENCIL D)

FLOWER DESIGN REPEAT (STENCILS E AND F)

LAUREL CORNER DESIGN (STENCILS E AND G OR H)

LEAF AND DOT STRIPE (STENCILS F AND G OR H)

REPEAT PATTERN (STENCIL E)

ROTATED DESIGN (STENCILS G OR H)

REFLECTED LAUREL BORDER (STENCIL E)

FLOWING RIBBON (STENCILS C OR D)

VICTORIAN BORDER

A traditional Victorian stylized flower design is brought up to date with the use of colour. A very pale lilac paint has been applied over a deeper shade of the same colour. A large flower is used as a corner or end piece to the pattern and the design can work in any direction from this point. A striped wall would look very pretty and you could, of course, reverse the colours and use the darker colour for the stencilling. The sponge roller technique makes this a very quick and easy project to complete.

PAINT COLOUR GUIDE

Pale lilac

SPONGING YOUR STENCIL

1 Paint the whole wall using deep lilac emulsion paint.

2 Use a plumb line and spirit level to mark the wall horizontally and vertically where you want the centre of each border to run. Draw a line through the centre of each stencil card design to match the position.

3 Starting with the large flower motifs (stencil A), use a sponge roller to apply the paint through the stencil and leave to dry.

4 When the design is complete, lightly sand the wall with a fine grade paper.

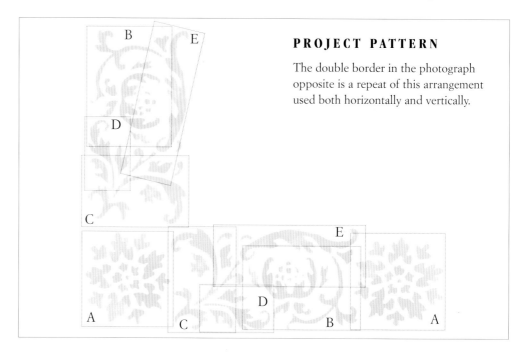

PROJECT PATTERN

The double border in the photograph opposite is a repeat of this arrangement used both horizontally and vertically.

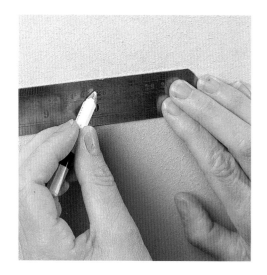

WORKING OUT THE POSITION OF YOUR STENCIL
The layout of the design can be adjusted, leaving a slightly larger gap between the central flower motif and the rest of the design to make sure that there is room for a flower in each corner. Work out approximately how many repeats will fit the area in between, then divide this number into the area exactly. Mark the position where the centre of the flowers will be placed.

USING A SPONGE ROLLER
Once the central flower motifs are in place, use the sponge roller to apply paint to the remaining sections of the design either side of these. Roller off excess paint onto kitchen paper so that it does not seep under the stencil.

SOFTENING YOUR STENCIL
You can soften the edges of the stencil and achieve a slightly worn and faded effect by rubbing the design with a very fine grade of sandpaper or finishing paper.

VICTORIAN BORDER VARIATIONS

Dark greens, blues and burgundy shades used to be extremely popular with the Victorians and you could try experimenting with the stencils in these colours. They tend to look particularly good in richly decorated dining rooms. Lighter colours are sometimes more appropriate in modern homes and the soft lilac colour scheme in the main project has been extended to include pastel pinks and greens.

REFLECTED LEAVES BORDER (STENCILS C AND D)

LARGE FLOWER REPEAT PATTERN (STENCIL A)

LARGE LEAF FRIEZE (STENCIL C)

FLOWERS WITHOUT CENTRE (STENCIL A WITH MASKED OFF CENTRE)

FLORAL BORDER DESIGN (STENCIL B)

REPEAT PATTERN (STENCIL D)

ALL-OVER LEAF DESIGN (STENCIL D)

FLORAL CORNER DESIGN (CENTRE OF STENCIL A)

FLOWING REFLECTED LEAVES WITH FLORAL DESIGN (CENTRE OF STENCIL A AND STENCIL E)

FLOWING REFLECTED LEAVES (STENCIL E)

SHADED AND REFLECTED LEAF STRIPE (STENCIL E)

SHADED LEAF DESIGN (STENCIL D)

SUPPLIERS

A. S. Handover
37 Mildmay Grove
London N1 4RH (Tel: 0207 359 4696)

Green and Stone
259 Kings Road
Chelsea
London SW3 5EL (Tel: 0207 352 0837)

Stencil Store Company Ltd
20–21 Heronsgate Road
Chorleywood
Hertfordshire WD3 5BN
.(Tel: 01923 285 577/88)

London Graphic Centre
16–18 Shelton Street
London WC2H 9JJ (Tel: 0207 240 0095)

ACKNOWLEDGEMENTS

First published in 2000 by Merehurst Limited
Ferry House, 51–57 Lacy Road, Putney, London SW15 1PR

© Copyright 2000 Merehurst Limited

ISBN 1-85391-882 2

Commissioning Editors: Natasha Martyn-Johns and Anna Sanderson
Project Editor: Anna Nicholas
Senior Designer: Helen Taylor
Photographer: Graeme Ainscough
Stylist: Caroline Davis
Publishing Manager: Fia Fornari
Production Manager: Lucy Byrne
CEO & Publisher: Anne Wilson
UK Marketing & Sales Director: Kathryn Harvey
International Sales Director: Kevin Lagden

Colour separation by Colourscan, Singapore
Printed in Singapore by Imago

Maggie Philo is a designer with many years experience working with a wide variety of decorative paint
finishes for walls and furniture. She is an experienced teacher of paint effects and other techniques including
gilding, stencilling and découpage. In 1993 she began selling her unique range of découpaged designs at major
fairs including the Country Living Fair, the House and Garden Fair, and the Homes and Gardens Grand Sales.
Maggie is the author of eight books, including *Decorative Painted Furniture* and regularly contributes to
homecraft magazines. She has also appeared on daytime television programmes demonstrating decorative
techniques, made a video, and given talks and demonstrations at numerous exhibitions and events.